PRAYING THE
GREAT
O ANTIPHONS

PRAYING THE GREAT O ANTIPHONS

My Soul Magnifies the Lord

KATY CARL

All booklets are published
thanks to the generosity of the supporters
of the Catholic Truth Society

All rights reserved. First published 2021 by The Incorporated Catholic Truth Society, 42-46 Harleyford Road, London SE11 5AY. Tel: 020 7640 0042. © 2021 The Incorporated Catholic Truth Society.
www.ctsbooks.org

ISBN 978 1 78469 661 0

CONTENTS

Praying Our Way to Christmas

This book exists to walk you through the text and context of the O Antiphons, which are prayed between 17th and 23rd December. In the space of about a week, we will read these short prayers together as a way of preparing ourselves to celebrate Christmas "in spirit and in truth." Since the end of Advent is a busy season for so many, this book is focused and limited, as it centres on an encounter with the words of the prayer and with images that illumine its meaning. The hope is that this meditative approach will bring readers into closer relation with Christ whose birth gives us such joy.

What is an antiphon?

An antiphon is a refrain, or repeated line, in prayer or song. In Christian prayer, antiphons frame text from the Psalms. Antiphons work to focus the attention and draw out important themes in prayer. The antiphon changes according to the day and season. It is commonly heard at Mass and during the *Liturgy of the Hours*. (For a deeper understanding of this Catholic prayer practice if it is unfamiliar to you, please see the section headed "How to Use These Texts".)

What are the O Antiphons?

These are seven short texts that the Church prays every year as the season of Advent draws to a close. The "O" in these antiphons is *vocative*: from the Latin *vocare*, to call. Each individual text is a cry, an *invocation*, welling up from humanity's desire for God. Each text, too, includes hints and glimmers of God's desire for humanity. Each one calls upon God – most urgently upon Jesus, God the Son, the second person of the Holy Trinity – to draw closer to us, to guide us, to lead us, to save us.

Taken together, the O Antiphons tell a story of how God, taking action in history, in our lives, and at the end of time, does exactly what these prayers ask him to do: he comes to us, dwells with us, invites us into his own life, and sets us free. Starting in our existential response to the mystery of creation, and leading us through a recapitulation of salvation history, the antiphons culminate with the feast of Christmas, when Jesus answers our prayer by coming to earth as a baby boy; by living a full human life on earth; and finally by allowing himself to be handed over to death for our salvation, only to rise again.

If this were only a story, in the sense of myth, legend, or fairy tale, occurring in the liminal space of 'once upon a time,' we might say of it what Flannery O'Connor notoriously said of the Eucharist: "Well, if it's only a symbol, to hell with it". But as O'Connor knew well, the Eucharist is not only a symbol: it truly is the Body, Blood, Soul, and Divinity of

God the Son, the second person of the Holy Trinity. And the story of the birth of Christ is not only a symbol, either. It *is* the Word of God, alive in us to the extent we are alive in Christ. It took place first in history, it was recorded in Scripture, and through the mystery of baptism it becomes embedded in each of our individual lives and circumstances. It plays itself out anew in human life again and again. Once our eyes are opened to it, we will begin to see it everywhere.

The O Antiphons ask God to open our eyes to this mystery. As such, they are the kind of prayer that we need to pray much more than God needs to hear it from us. We pray these antiphons, we sing them, we call out in them, to acknowledge our insatiable need for God and our inexhaustible gratitude to God for meeting that need. They are the kind of prayer in which, if we call out to God and then listen closely, we can begin to hear God's responding, and responsive, call to us.

A Word on the Subtitle

Alert readers will notice that this book's subtitle, "My soul magnifies the Lord," does not appear anywhere in the O Antiphons themselves. Instead it comes directly from the *Magnificat*, Mary's great hymn of praise and glory to God. In contrast to the O Antiphons, which are prayed only in the week before Christmas, the Church prays the *Magnificat* daily. This hymn forms part of the stable, unchanging core of Evening Prayer in the *Liturgy of the Hours*.

Though other parts of that Liturgy vary with the season and the feast, just as the Propers of the Mass do, the *Magnificat* remains the same day after day. In all times and in all circumstances, the Church finds it "right and just" to speak with Mary's voice. One of the cornerstones of our common liturgical life is built, then, on a woman's words. True, not just any woman, and not just any words: Mary is the *Theotokos*, bearer of God. She bears God into the world not in the limited and secondary ways all believers do, not even in the literal way priests sacramentally do when they confect the Eucharist, but in a way that is unique in all human history. She bore God himself into the world in the human body that he took on in the Incarnation.

Catholics also believe that Mary is the Immaculate Conception, meaning she was created from her own beginning without Original Sin. *Theotokos*, Mother of God, Immaculate Conception; these are titles no other human, male or female, can legitimately carry: just as no other human can claim, as Christ could, to be fully God and fully human. Contemplating these truths about Mary and Jesus often highlights our distance from them.

At the same time, through grace Mary and Jesus, for all of their uniqueness, live close to us – closer, at times, than we are to ourselves. The extraordinary work of grace in Mary's life and words can transform us even in its most ordinary aspects. Mary is the prime example of nature transfigured by grace. In her, grace is built on nature to the peak of human possibility, so that her voice uniquely has power to speak for all humanity. She is, for created humanity, the "prime example of sonship".[1] She embodies total self-gift in docility to the will of God. Though the saints sing of her perfect kindness and gentleness and mercy, she is not just "obedient" to anyone who wants something from her. Instead, her obedience belongs totally and unshakably to God, and all else that she does follows from that commitment. In this way, she models the total integrity that marks devotion, discipleship, and transformation in God. Only Christ could be both fully God and fully human, but being himself, he could show us how to live God's life, but he could not both be himself and show us how to follow himself. Mary, by contrast, shows us how to be fully human and fully God's: she shows us how to follow Christ.

This is why we speak her words daily, every evening, in the communal, universal prayer of the Church throughout time. This is why it is worth seeking to make her words our own. This is why, especially in these last days of Advent, it is fitting that "as we wait in joyful hope for the coming of our saviour" we speak, we pray, with the forceful and urgent cries of a labouring woman. I believe we can best hear what the O Antiphons seek to communicate to us if we hear them spoken in Mary's voice, as her cries and as the prophetic cries of the Church labouring to bring forth Christ into the world:

---

[1] "How Is God Our Father?" Fr John Baptist Ku, O.P., Thomistic Institute lecture at the Dominican House of Studies, 15th July 2020.

> For a long time I have kept silent,
> I have said nothing, holding myself back;
> now I cry out like a woman in labour,
> gasping and panting. (*Isa* 42:14)

This Scriptural simile, imaging a woman's cries in childbirth, is Isaiah's rendition of God's voice speaking to humanity. Yet in it, we can also hear an echo of words that might be spoken by Mary in her full freedom and co-operation with God's plan to bring the Son Incarnate into the world to offer salvation to all. According to Scripture scholar Michael Pakaluk, such "overtones" of Mary's voice can be found everywhere in the Gospel of John.[2] This makes abundant sense, as John's spiritual life was necessarily influenced by having Mary live in his home for decades after the events of Jesus's bodily life on earth, communicating with her daily and treasuring along with her the memories of Christ's early years, ministry, Passion, Death, and Resurrection. Surely, beginning at the feast of Pentecost, the voice of Mary's daily prayer would have similarly influenced the Apostles as they co-operated to establish the earliest liturgies. After all, Mary was in a unique way the 'bride' of the Holy Spirit, and the whole Church mirrors her in this role in prayer. So perhaps Marian "overtones" may also be found in the liturgy, in places we may easily recognise them as well as in places we may not have thought to look.

---

[2] Michael Pakaluk, *Mary's Voice in the Gospel According to John: A New Translation with Commentary* (Washington, DC: Regnery Gateway, 2021).

The O Antiphons may, then, provide us with a privileged opportunity to hear Mary's voice at prayer. If so, then as Mary is the model for all discipleship of Christ, we will do well to listen to her language in every nuance of its diction and intonation. In doing so, we will draw closer to the spirit of her Son, which gives every believer power to become like him (*John* 1:12-13). She will then speak for us in prayer, if we will allow her to do so. This is the true nature of the Marian dimension of authority within the Church, equally accessible to all believers: Mary's power derives from her total alignment with the fullness of God's Providence, in every detail and in every particular of life. In praying with her, we too align ourselves to this Providence, to every good gift our loving God wants to give us, to the wonders he has created and wants to continue creating, among us, moment by moment and day after day.

A Word on Perspective

Aristotle writes that whatever we perceive, we perceive the way we do because of the kind of creature we are. What kind of person we already are will influence what seems good to us, what interests us, what we desire, what we love.[3] This book bears the marks of that reality. I write not as a scholar of theology or Scripture, not as one who is ordained or consecrated, but simply as a Catholic laywoman who also happens to be a writer of fiction and nonfiction, an editor,

---

[3] See Aristotle, *Nicomachean Ethics*, Book I.

an erstwhile teacher, a wife (of a philosopher, hence the Aristotle), and the mother of a young, noisy family. My experience, then, will colour my understanding and my communication. Readers' own experiences will similarly colour what they can receive from these words. At the same time, I work from a core understanding that all people, whatever the markers of their identity, are called to holiness,[4] which is more than mere human 'wholeness', but is instead real glorification, unity with God.

Even writing the word 'God' opens up a whole host of issues and questions. Whether we understand who and what we are talking about when we talk about God is its own question. Whether we can ever really understand this, to what degree we can understand it, is another, separate question. I don't assume that everyone who picks up this book will have had a similar experience of the language of divine revelation. I don't even assume that every reader will be Catholic or that those who are Catholic will already have a thorough knowledge of the Church's traditional practices and teachings. None of us is born with this knowledge. For most of us, even for 'cradle Catholics' like me it takes the work of decades to build up a framework of Catholic thought and praxis. I do take it as read, however, that by 'God' is meant the Father of all existence who made all things, loves all things, holds all things in being; the Son who echoes and

---

[4] See Vatican Council II, *Lumen Gentium* (Dogmatic Constitution on the Church), no 39.

embodies the love of the Father by his entrance into creation to save, cleanse, and heal it; and the Holy Spirit, the active love of the Father and the Son, operating throughout all of creation and all of time.

God in this sense has a story, expressed through event and action, not in the sense of fiction but of history. He is at the same time, and no less so, beyond all history and above all human comprehension. This paradox – the Ultimate becoming minuscule, the Abstract concrete, the Infinite finite – is the central mystery we will be thinking about together in this book. It has the flavour of myth or fairy tale, but this is no wishful thinking, no fabrication: it is what C.S. Lewis called "Myth become Fact," about which his friend J.R.R. Tolkien had the following to say:

> The Birth of Christ is the eucatastrophe* of Man's history. The Resurrection is the eucatastrophe of the story of the Incarnation. This story begins and ends in joy. It has pre-eminently "the inner consistency of reality." There is no tale ever told that men would rather find was true, and none which so many sceptical men have accepted as true on its own merits. For the Art of it has the supremely convincing tone of Primary Art, that is, of Creation. To reject it leads either to sadness or to wrath.[5]

---

* This word is, as far as I can discover, of Tolkien's coinage. By it he means a cataclysmic, transformative, but overwhelmingly joyous conclusive event of a narrative: much more than a mere "happy ending".

[5] J.R.R. Tolkien, "On Fairy-stories," in *The Tolkien Reader* (New York: Ballantine, 1966), 72.

Part of the uniqueness of Christianity is that it offers this inexhaustibly fascinating and rich poetic metaphor, capable of ceaselessly entrancing the mind. Yet at the same time, it presents this truth in a tale simple enough for any child to grasp and accept: God loved everyone; everyone was in trouble; to save us, God needed to be united with human nature. God came to Mary to ask if she would help him take on a human nature. Mary said yes, and so God became a baby and was born in a stable in a city of ancient Judah, in the ancient Roman Empire. He did this, not 'once upon a time,' but in either the year 6 or 7 BC, during the time when Caesar Augustus was the Roman emperor and Herod was king of Judea.

That it is so easy to tell just this story in just this way to our children can at times deceive us into thinking it is a story only fit for children. Yet all the time we are telling it, it is involving us in the deepest philosophical and theological questions. In service to that depth, where I cannot descend with the ease that scholars do, this book will pursue simplicity. We will walk through this story together as it deserves to be told: slowly, reverently, detail by detail and stage by stage.

How to Use These Texts

As I mentioned in the Introduction, the O Antiphons have their origin in the way the Church prays the Mass and the *Liturgy of the Hours*. If you are already familiar with these practices, please feel free to skip to the short list of suggestions below. This longer explanation is included for your benefit if you are one of the following:

- A newly baptised Catholic still learning about the traditions and prayers of the Church
- Someone interested in the Church, but not ready to commit to receiving the Sacraments
- A Catholic who is new to praying the traditional texts of the Church
- Anyone who is seeking a way to enter into contemplative prayer

Catholic public prayer has its roots in the practices of the first Jews who became Christians. These believers met daily to chant shared songs and rituals together, especially the Psalms. (Some early Christian communities chanted all 150 Psalms together every day!) As time went on, the order of public prayers took on its own form and its own seasonality. The pattern followed the natural year: at the darkest season, Christians celebrated the return of light – and Light – to the world with the birth of Jesus Christ.

Catholic public prayer is characterised by its communal nature. This shared character is reflected in the word *liturgy*, stemming from a Greek root that means "public work." The Church observes two major liturgical cycles: the Holy Sacrifice of the Mass and the *Liturgy of the Hours*. For each of these cycles, each day of each year has its own designated texts. The Church may offer many different sets of texts to choose from, depending on the occasion, the liturgical season and the place in the Lectionary, which gives the full three-year cycle of Mass readings.

The *Liturgy of the Hours*, also called the Divine Office, is a practice of Christian prayer, rooted in Jewish origins, in which participants chant the Psalms, sing hymns, and read aloud from texts of Scripture and Tradition. The letters of the New Testament, and readings from early Christian monks and scholars, figure largely in these text selections.

This Liturgy traditionally consists in seven parts or "hours," in fulfilment of the scriptural text "Seven times day I praise you" (*Ps* 119:164):

Lauds (dawn prayer)
Matins or Prime (morning prayer)
Terce (midmorning prayer: the third hour in medieval timekeeping)
Sext (midday prayer: the sixth hour)
None (mid-afternoon prayer: the ninth hour)
Vespers (evening prayer)
Compline (night prayer, often said just before sleep)

A shortened, contemporary version of the Liturgy contains the Office of Readings, Morning Prayer, Daytime Prayer (which compresses the three midday hours into one), Evening Prayer, and Night Prayer.

The full text of the *Liturgy of the Hours* is contained in the Breviary, which is commonly published either as a four-volume set or as a single, compressed book. You can also access the text through websites like *DivineOffice.org* or apps like *iBreviary* (which I use and recommend).

Priests promise to pray the *Liturgy of the Hours* daily as part of the responsibilities of their ordination. The *Liturgy of the Hours* gives shape and substance to the community life of consecrated men and women and enriches the prayer life of individuals and families worldwide.

The practice is not required for laypeople, for whom this book is primarily intended. And, of course, you need not pray the *Liturgy of the Hours* in order to pray the O Antiphons. All of the above is offered mainly as context. Still, many find that praying even one hour, such as Morning Prayer or Vespers, anchors and focuses their days, expands their knowledge of the Word of God, and strengthens their connection to Christ and his Church.

Whether you do so regularly or occasionally, alone or in community, it is worth learning how to pray the *Liturgy of the Hours*. And if you have never prayed it in community with other Christians, whether at someone's home, in church, or in a religious house like a monastery or convent, it is well worth making the effort to pursue this experience. Most monasteries practice hospitality. Even many cloistered communities maintain common areas in their churches, where visitors are welcome. If unfamiliarity makes you hesitant about paying a visit, call ahead for details. The overwhelming majority of communities will be delighted to know of your interest and to welcome you into this aspect of their shared prayer life.

The *Liturgy of the Hours* can seem complicated to beginners, but it need not be daunting. As with building any habit, it is more than all right to start with a small piece of the whole and add on from there. For anyone who desires detailed guidance on how to make the *Liturgy of the Hours* a regular part of a family's routine, I highly recommend a resource called *The Little Oratory: A Beginner's Guide to Praying in the Home* by David Clayton and Leila Lawler (Sophia Institute Press, 2014).

For now, all you really need to know is that in this book, for each reflection, you will see two texts: the Gospel Acclamation and the *Magnificat* Antiphon. The Gospel Acclamation is prayed once during Mass as a line of song or chant during the Liturgy of the Word, just before the Gospel is read aloud. The *Magnificat* Antiphon is prayed during Evening Prayer, between sections from the Psalms.

If you are praying the prayers of the Mass as well as the *Liturgy of the Hours*, you will hear both texts during the course of the day. For personal devotion and reflection, you may refer to either text, or both, as you prefer. Most of the reflections in this book draw on both texts.

If you don't have the opportunity to attend Mass or pray the *Liturgy of the Hours* most days, here are some ways you might incorporate the O Antiphons into a personal or family prayer practice. Many of these ideas can serve you even if you are extremely short on spare time, but, if you feel moved to devote more time despite a busy schedule, don't immediately assume it is impossible: "for nothing will be impossible with God" (*Luke* 1:37). Advent is all about how God's reality can break into our time, creating space where we did not expect to find it.

Prayerfully consider whether you might do one or more of the following:

- Add the O Antiphon before or after your usual morning or evening prayer.

- Add the text to your usual prayer when saying grace before the main meal of the day.

- Read the O Antiphon aloud when lighting your Advent wreath, if you use one.

- Practice *Lectio Divina* with the O Antiphon: find a quiet moment to sit alone with the text. Read it slowly, consider the meaning, and pay close attention to what the language is really saying. Read it again, and let the Holy Spirit speak to you in the words.

- Put up an image of the Nativity where you will see it often during your work, and take a moment between tasks to re-read the text of the day's O Antiphon while looking at the image.

• Make your own poem, visual art, narrative, or other creative reflection in response to one or more of the O Antiphon texts.

• Take this book with you into a Catholic chapel or church near your home or work, and simply spend a few moments enjoying the art and the prayers.

O Sapientia

Gospel Acclamation:
Wisdom of the Most High, ordering all things with strength and gentleness, come and teach us the way of truth.

Magnificat Antiphon:
O Wisdom, you come forth from the mouth of the Most High. You fill the universe and hold all things together in a strong yet gentle manner. O come teach us the way of truth.

1534 OVR LADY OF WALSINGHAM, PRAY FOR VS 1934

Reflection:

The central image of the story of Christmas is the image of Mary holding the newborn Christ under the star in Bethlehem. We do not tend to think of a newborn as inspiring terror and awe. Yet many parents report the experience of total wonder at the birth of a child as nothing less than cataclysmic. This experience can bring a complete reconstruction of our way of seeing the world, a radical rearrangement of priorities. In this way it is not unlike our experience of turning towards God and beginning to centre our lives on him rather than on ourselves. In a world not particularly welcoming to new life, both experiences can seem like an illustration of the way in which "the wisdom of this world is folly with God" (*1 Cor* 3:19). Still, even many nonbelievers recognise the necessity, for a happy life, of living for a purpose beyond our own pleasure and satisfaction.

We see ourselves correctly when we see ourselves as essentially small in proportion to the rest of the world: not insignificant, not worthless, but not the centre of all things, either. Many people have this experience for the first time when facing a monumental task that both offers great joy and demands full attention: a life's work. This perspective characterises the voice of Mary's *Magnificat*, in which she looks at herself and at the work of God in relation to one another. Although her role is undeniably, overwhelmingly great, the highest given to any human ever born, she sees herself as essentially small – not bad, not meaningless, but *small* – in relation to the broader story in which she is participating. This is what our tradition means by humility; it is also the beginning of what our tradition means by wisdom.

This perspective is also the genius of St Thérèse of Lisieux's "little way," which allows us to see our human business and human preoccupations as at once deeply important to ourselves and to God – as important as the details of a child's life to a good parent – and at the same time pallid in significance beside the grand scheme of the cosmos. A perspective like this allows us, in the popular phrase, to "pray as though it all depends on God and work as though it all depends on us," while also holding our lives with a light touch, ready to let go of what God wants us to surrender when it is no longer ours to hold.

To see ourselves this way, in right perspective and right relation with the rest of creation, also places us into relation with the wisdom of God who made us as we are. In the Catholic tradition, created wisdom is personified in the Book of Proverbs. Chapter 8 enters into the point of view of this person as it speaks in a voice attributed to Wisdom (8:24-26, 29-31):

> When there were no depths I was brought forth,
> when there were no springs abounding with water.
> Before the mountains had been shaped,
> before the hills, I was brought forth,
> before he had made the earth with its fields,
> or the first of the dust of the world…

When he marked out the foundations of the earth,
then I was beside him, like a master workman,
and I was daily his delight,
rejoicing in his inhabited world
and delighting in the children of man.

Who is the speaker here? The verse has been taken in different contexts to refer to Christ, the "master workman" "without whom was made nothing that was made" (cf. *John* 1), but many saints have associated the speaker's voice here with Mary's voice, as well. This speaks to the close co-operation of Jesus and Mary in the work of the Incarnation. It supports the thought that Mary was present in the divine plan for salvation from its inception. God chose to ask the consent of a woman to give him his humanity, in a unique meeting of the natural and supernatural orders, rather than to arrange this creation for himself in some other way, as he certainly could have done.

That created wisdom is personified in the Psalms and thus in the Catholic tradition as female tends to strengthen this interpretation. God is pure spirit, existing beyond gender: although in a way it is proper to speak of him as masculine, this is only an analogy. In himself, God contains and creates and provides all the perfections of every human person without exception, male and female, as all are made in his image (cf. *Gen* 1:27). And while God the Son undoubtedly came to earth as a human male, in his identity as Divine Wisdom he transcends his human nature without destroying or denying it. He already contains in himself the source of all the graces given to Mary to empower her to become the mother of the Word Incarnate. Both Mary and Christ are, in different senses, the model for all who desire to give themselves fully to God.

Human wisdom's fullest expression is found in this self-gift, in our openness to the meeting of nature with grace. Divine Wisdom picks up the thread here, as it takes in hand the whole picture of our lives: what we can control and what we cannot, what is given to us to accept and what is given to us to change, from the beginning of time to its end, and spanning the whole of the cosmos. The original Latin text of this antiphon reflects this aspect of wisdom: it reaches '*a fine usque ad finem*,' 'from end to end,' ordering all things '*fortiter suavitate*'–'mightily and sweetly.'[6] Hold on to these two ideas: both the thought of the totality of God's ambit and the thought of how God unites power with beauty, order with awe.

For now, we can observe that we traditionally associate wisdom not only with Christ but also with the life and person of Mary, especially under her title Our Lady, Seat of Wisdom. This title evokes images of Mary holding the infant Jesus as well as depictions of the Pietà, the moment when the crucified Jesus is taken down from the Cross and his body is given to Mary to hold one last time. Not only

---

[6] My gratitude is due here to Brian Carl for these translations from the Latin.

in these literal senses, though, is Mary truly said to be the Seat of Wisdom, as the one person who was most especially given God's human nature to care for and love in the order of nature as well as of grace. In whom she is, in who God made her to be, Mary incarnates created, human wisdom; she instantiates it. Her wisdom lives both in what she says and in what she does.

To see this reality in action, think of Mary "travelling in haste" to the hill country of Judah to be with Elizabeth for the birth of John the Baptist. This journey showed Mary's exercise of agency and her innate practical wisdom. Caryll Houselander describes the surprising nature of Mary's decision in this way:

> Many women, if they were expecting a child, would refuse to hurry over the hills on a visit of pure kindness. They would say they had a duty to themselves and to their unborn child which came before anything or anyone else.
>
> The Mother of God considered no such thing… Although Mary's own child was God, she could not forget Elizabeth's need – almost incredible to us, but characteristic of her.[7]

This concern for the other is characteristic, too, of Christ, who at this point in the story is incarnate already in Mary's womb and who has saved Mary from Original Sin by a special grace. Houselander explains that in this moment,

---

[7] Caryll Houselander, *The Reed of God* (Notre Dame, IN: Ave Maria Press, 2020), 47.

we see Christ's action in Mary's: her will in his and his will in hers. Her free decision is enlivened and encouraged by Christ's presence and that of the Holy Spirit. When we are aligned to the will and wisdom of God, our lives can mirror this dynamic, as Houselander writes:

> If Christ is growing in us, if we are at peace, recollected, because we know that however insignificant our life seems to be, from it He is forming Himself; if we go with eager wills, "in haste," to wherever our circumstances compel us, because we believe that He desires to be in that place, we shall find that we are driven more and more to act on the impulse of His love.
>
> And the answer we shall get from others to those impulses will be an awakening into life, or the leap into joy of the already wakened life within them.[8]

This readiness to act boldly, with reason and justice, when called by life and love, has its root in Mary's deeper spiritual wisdom: in her recognition of her smallness balanced against the greatness of God. And it is no accident that, in the middle of this practical journey, Mary will deliver her great spiritual text, the *Magnificat*.

Notice that, in the *Magnificat*, Mary does not talk about how worthless or how insignificant she is; on the contrary, the line feels almost like a boast: "All generations will call

---

[8] Caryll Houselander, *The Reed of God* (Notre Dame, IN: Ave Maria Press, 2020), 48.

me blessed, for he who is mighty has done great things for me" (*Luke* 1:48-49). Yet most of the poem, for we can call it that, is not about Mary at all but about God. Mary describes the action God is beginning to take in and through her, which he will continue beyond and beside her, and which will eventually fill all of creation. The *Magnificat*, then, tells a story about salvation history, as expressed in the life of Mary. The O Antiphons, in their way, also tell this story, as expressed in the life of God's people, in his covenants, and in the Church.

Mary's preparation to receive Christ has been, first of all, a spiritual preparation. In one sense, she has been preparing for it her whole life. Tradition tells us that she was conceived without sin, that Anne and Joachim were the parents of a child who had received a completely unprecedented grace, totally unique in history (and I don't know what will make you a saint faster than parenting a child who is totally unique in history). Next, tradition also has it that from early childhood, Mary spent time being educated in the Temple; she would have been deeply familiar with the Scriptures. St Augustine tells us that she conceived Christ in her heart and mind before she conceived him in her body. Her education blossomed into her *yes* to God at the Annunciation.

In the great hymn of the *Magnificat*, whose tones will influence how we read the O Antiphons in this book, we hear Mary's voice: profoundly original and yet deeply formed by what has come before her. Her hymn draws on the voices of women in Scripture, particularly on the speeches of Eve, Sarah, Hannah – those women who did not expect to give birth but who were surprised with a child by the grace of God. Yet what Mary says, like the manner of her conception of Jesus, is completely new. With total justice, she makes claims no other woman of the Chosen People has been able to make. The impossible has become possible for Mary not only because of her faith but also because of her reason:

> Her inner life was crucial: her consent, above all, to the divine plan, to bear a child, but also her possession of the intellectual virtues – thoughtfulness, wisdom, understanding – that made that consent possible. In the face of everyday pressures and demands to the contrary, she chooses the most important things. Therefore her image was drawn to reflect the highest development of a human being, humanity in its full dignity and splendour, an actor at the crucial moment in the history of the world who was at the same time held up as a model for anyone to imitate.[9]

And if Elizabeth had not been there to hear and receive the words in which Mary celebrates God's wisdom, her own consent, and God's reciprocal, superabundant response,

---

[9]   Zena Hitz, *Lost in Thought: The Hidden Pleasures of an Intellectual Life* (Princeton/Oxford: Princeton University Press, 2020). Hitz identifies this idea, of Mary's human wisdom as a precondition of her receptivity to the Divine Incarnation, as having come first from the scriptural commentaries of Origen; St Augustine also famously endorses it.

how would these words ever have been recorded? To her active receptivity, too, we owe one of the greatest prayers Scripture has given.

On the purely practical side, Mary would have learned from her visit to Elizabeth what she could expect in childbirth, the stages of labour for which she would need to prepare her mind and body, and the supplies she would need to carry with her: blankets, linens, the swaddling clothes we hear about in the Gospel of Luke. (Could these clothes have been John's newborn hand-me-downs?) Remember that she and Joseph were starting out together on a worker's wages. They could not afford thoughtless spontaneities. They would have talked and worked and planned together to be ready for the child's arrival. They would have trusted in Providence, yes, but this very trust would have driven them to be *provident*, an old word expressing a sense of care and diligence. Their practical preparation would have been lending itself to a deeper spiritual preparation.

Next, when she received the news of the requirement to travel for the census, Mary must have begun thinking about the journey to Bethlehem. She must have packed supplies; she must have planned on a place to stay. She likely had reason to trust that it would be simple to find space. How else would a woman, nine months pregnant, approach travelling near her due date? Yet, again, Mary does not exempt herself from the common lot, or ask God (as most of us surely would ask God) to spare her the journey.

This transition is where the story turns towards surprise. That we all know it turned out just as prophecy predicted, and as we feel it should – the Holy Family being refused room at the inn, the Christ Child's birth in a stable – can obscure this surprise. Many writers point to the contrast between the dignity and glory of Jesus, the Son of God, and the humble, gritty setting of the story of his human birth. Still more surprising is that the Seat of Wisdom was, despite her best planning, faced with the unexpected. Here Mary shines as a model of what we are to do when human wisdom has done all it can do. At this stage, divine wisdom must be invited to take over, and divine wisdom is always a gift, a grace.

Practical wisdom, in the Catholic tradition, also carries the name *phronesis* or prudence. Here I would like to reclaim the word "prudence" from some ill-deserved negative cultural associations. Many people tend to think the word implies either prudery, a fearful shrinking from facts and details, or else an excessive and self-absorbed caution that fails to account for the goodness of creation and the love of God. Instead, prudence is simply an ability to do the things that bring peace to our existence. In prudence, knowledge meets ability; being meets doing. Prudence takes what is given and turns it into what is both possible and beneficial for human life. Prudence lends itself to our full flourishing.

No question, this is one reason why Mary, as well as being called the Seat of Wisdom, is also called the Queen of Peace:

because of her ability to perform acts and habits shaped by wisdom, to relate human wisdom to divine wisdom, and to help us form these same tendencies in ourselves. Most of all, she carries these titles because she brings us into relation with the source of all wisdom, of all peace: Christ himself. "The fear of the Lord is the beginning of wisdom" (*Prov* 9:10). This fear should not be taken as aversion or horror, but as the awestruck wonder that floods the nerves and splits open the hearts of new parents. The attitude suggested by this image of a mother lost in adoring wonder before the marvellous reality of a newborn is a good one to carry with us as we approach these days of intense preparation for Christmas. God accepts us just the way the mother accepts the newborn, in this way may he teach us to accept him when he comes to us as a human child.

O Adonai

Gospel Acclamation:
Ruler of the House of Israel, who gave the law to Moses on Sinai, come and save us with outstretched arm.

Magnificat Antiphon:
O Adonai and leader of Israel, you appeared to Moses in a burning bush and you gave him the Law on Sinai. O come and save us with your mighty power.

Reflection:

The thought that a newborn could become the king of anything at all is, historically, an unsettling idea. An adult would need to rule in the child's place, thus threatening the line of succession and, by extension, the whole political order. Yet from the moment of Jesus's birth, we hail him as the Ruler of the House of Israel, the lawgiver of all human life. Although on one level we can now recognise this antiphon immediately for what it is – a welcome of Jesus Christ's deepest identity as God – it would have been by no means intuitive to the senses if we were observers at the Nativity. We might have wanted to take the wise men aside and ask them: What on earth are you doing? What use does a newborn have for a king's treasury? Likewise, the shepherds: Why are you singing and crying, in the middle of the night, no less? It's just a poor woman's baby. Pipe down, can't you? We're trying to sleep. Their homage makes sense only if we recognise, as they instantly did, Jesus's inherent authority and regency. But if we shift our point of view, if we put ourselves in the place of a common person of the time, for example of the innkeeper who refused the Holy Family a place, the scene becomes very strange indeed.

Then again, we may not need to travel back in history through Ignatian meditation to find unfamiliar, challenging, ideas in this antiphon. Though we are accustomed to the idea of a monarch as a symbol of authority and even to some extent a guide for a country, the idea of a ruler as powerful and influential frequently lacks the resonance for us that it had for premodern societies. So we will need to think more fully about the idea of kingship. Living in a postmodern world, we can be hesitant, even highly averse, towards the idea of answering to a higher authority than our autonomous selves or a democratic political order. Many consider divine authority either notional, a fairy tale cooked up by autocrats who want more control over others, or else like the loving but distant oversight of a long-deceased ancestor, not present or specific enough to affect anyone's daily life. If we think of unity, we often think of it as a phenomenon arising from the grassroots of society, not imposed upon us from the top down.

Revelation suggests another picture altogether, not a political picture but a spiritual one. Revelation tells of a God whose rulership was expressed in a life lived close to his people, in which he spoke to them and guided their hearts. This God made a highly specific demand of the first humans, a demand they chose directly and deliberately to dishonour. In declining to obey God, the giver of everything in our lives that is good, they brought about Original Sin. They severed themselves – and *all* of us – from the unity between himself and humanity that God originally intended. They created, on their own, this human need for salvation, whose urgency runs like an electrical current through the course of these seven days of preparation. We recreate this need for salvation every time we sin – which, unfortunately, is not rare.

In allowing Original Sin, in allowing our personal and individual sin, God honours human freedom as he created it. In seeking to heal the rift sin causes, God honours the human capacity for love he created in us. He wants us to turn to him freely, not just once, but as many times as necessary: not under force, not in blind ignorance, and not lawlessly, but like Mary, in the totality and fullness of our capacity for consent. His authority, in the formula of St Augustine, commands what it gives and gives what it commands. Like the form of a poem that shapes the poet's composition, it restricts only in order to liberate. Restraint, fully understood, is the scaffolding we climb to attain new heights. The title *Adonai* holds and implies all this: it is the name of a leader, a lawgiver, but one with a tender concern for the well-being of his people. He is not aloof or removed, but turned towards us, ready to hear and address our concerns.

Here again, we can allow ourselves to be startled by the contrast between the idea of the exalted "ruler of the house of Israel" and of the whole world – the Lawgiver, the Anointed One, the Chosen, the Messiah – and the image we began with: the picture of a powerless newborn lying swaddled on a cushion of straw. This image suggests vulnerability and, in that suggestion, adds still another layer of surprise. How is it that someone so clearly in need of saving – this child of a low-income family, born far from home, under a death threat from the king of his region – could ever be the Saviour? How does this helpless person act in union with the good Father on whose Providence we depend; how does this portrait of weakness become the Good Shepherd whose strength we can trust? That so few could possibly have seen or known or understood the divine irony at the time can only add to our wonder. This aspect of the story, the contrast between weakness and strength, beneficially destabilises our vision. It demands we look anew at St Paul's idea that God's "power is made perfect in weakness... For when I am weak, then I am strong" (*2 Cor* 12:9-10).

This idea can seem dissonant to the extent that the world around us either forbids us to acknowledge human vulnerability or else invites us to exploit it for our advantage. The hardest demand of all may be to locate ourselves within this idea of strength-in-weakness: to combine an awareness of the shared human condition, and an honesty about the ways in which we have suffered, with a clear and secure sense that we are the beloved children of God.

The question of whose stories are allowed to be heard, and whose pain deserves compassion, can pose an obstacle to this awareness. In order to see rightly, we need to know that God cares about every individual without exception. He is not pleased when we shout over each other or when we allow a cruel coldness the upper hand in our dealings with each other. If, in our cultural and personal history, we have lacked examples of figures who unite strength with gentleness, sway over others with authentic concern for those others' well-being, this can pose still another obstacle to understanding a good and loving God, who limits and shapes his own exercise of power for our benefit. He does not need to make extraordinary displays of force to evoke our acknowledgement of what he can do. He does not throw his weight around or make extravagant demands. In a word, the God of power and might does not behave the way that humans given power generally behave. His action is subtle, gentle, and infinitely patient.

This self-limitation of God reveals his mercy and our freedom, yet at times it can also create the feeling of an incomprehensible absence. Why does God seem not to act in certain situations? Why does he permit humans to cause certain harms that genuinely damage and legitimately outrage each other's dignity? Many saints have observed that God's action in such situations is not absent but is hidden from us as a kindness to our limited minds. Another way to look at this might be that God's action in other lives is often hidden from us as a protection of those souls' privacy. Many who have survived horrors report journeying out the other side of those experiences with a firmer, more complete sense of God's tender love in action, despite the reality of the suffering humans cause each other. Some of these experiences can be so interior and incommunicable that to demand an explanation is to demand the impossible.

So, instead of always needing to hold a perfect and clear comprehension of events – a need that often conceals a disguised desire to *control* those same events – we can learn to ask better questions. How can we imagine hearing the voice of God calling an abuser to repent of sins we cannot even conceive of wanting to commit, the very names of which cause pain? Can we even begin to hear how he might call a wounded soul to forgive in a voice that also grants that same power of forgiveness? How can we dare to say God is absent in a situation when we cannot fully know so many of the details of that situation, including the perspectives and inner lives of everyone involved – even when one of those perspectives is our own?

So self-knowledge, awareness of others, and under-standing of God walk hand in hand. Because of Original Sin, self-discovery is always a *re*discovery: a recovery of what has been lost. At the same time, this recovery is the doing of a God who can "create in me a clean heart" (*Ps* 51:10) and who says to us: "Behold, I am doing a new thing" (*Isa* 43:19). To rediscover who we are, we must also rediscover who God is. This is why the search for God's living and ever-new presence, implied in this prayer by the image of Moses facing the burning bush, is integrated with the idea of our burning need for a law and a Saviour. God's saving action at one and the same time returns us to the abundant joy of our origins and, within the limits of his justice, propels us forward into his project of creating anew. Any false opposition, any either/or, between these is missing some aspect of truth. We should not rest until we receive from God the clarity we long for about such missing pieces.

O Radix Jesse

Gospel Acclamation:
*Root of Jesse, set up as a sign to the peoples,
come to save us, and delay no more.*

Magnificat Antiphon:
*O stock of Jesse, you stand as a signal for the
nations; kings fall silent before you whom
the peoples acclaim. O come and deliver us,
and do not delay.*

Reflection:

We began this series with the idea that the O Antiphons tell a story. As we travel deeper into reflection and closer to the revelatory eucatastrophe of Christmas Day, we discover that the O Antiphons are telling us not one story but many stories, in many timelines. They lead us to consider the birth of Christ in history (a story of the past), the birth of Christ into our souls (a story of the present), and the birth of Christ into the Church (a story of past, present, and future). This antiphon points us towards the past, not to hold us there, but to help us all the better to understand the context into which Christ was born in time.

The mention of Jesse and his family line introduces the ideas of ancestry and prophecy into our understanding of who and what Jesus is. Both ideas, like that of kingship, challenge the postmodern mind. Rightly, we today tend to value all heritages equally and to be sceptical of anyone claiming to have a privileged message from God. There is justice in both of these modern tendencies: we do well to honour the truth that every human, of every race and colour, country and origin, bears God's image in absolute equality. We do well, too, to resist confident but baseless truth claims of every kind, evaluating words with care before granting our assent: "Test everything, hold fast what is good" (*1 Thes* 5:21).

However, the modern mind also tends to split spirit from body, an age-long damage which Christ came to reconcile. It tends to distance our heritage from our identity, to hold our flesh at arm's length from our mind. We sometimes think of this split as making us more intellectual or more rational, qualities our education leads us to see as praiseworthy. We also may think of the split as a way of avoiding the errors of our cultural baggage, in which physical or national differences have been abused as meretricious explanations for existing power imbalances or as ways to unjustly assert the dominance of some over others. Again, this desire is right to an extent. Cultural arrogance and the abuse of power can never please the God who "has scattered the proud in the thoughts of their hearts" and "has brought down the mighty from their thrones and exalted those of humble estate" (*Luke* 1:51-52). In calling attention to these truths, Mary's is the voice of a woman deeply rooted in the intellectual, historical, and spiritual tradition of her people, yet at the same time bursting forth with all the urgency and immediacy of the Holy Spirit's action in the present.

But what, then, is the antiphon saying? Or to ask it another way: How is God's having "helped his servant Israel" – which, remember, Mary and Jesus embody and instantiate, in their shared physical, historical, intellectual, and spiritual heritage – also "a signal to the nations" and a promise of God's salvation to the whole world? It is no contradiction in terms that Jesus's particular ancestry in this world is an expression of, not incidental or accidental to, his position as universal Saviour. The "root" or "stock of Jesse" means the house of King David. Scriptural prophecies in Isaiah predicted that the Messiah, the Saviour of the people, would come from this family line. Through Joseph's legal adoption of him, the child in Mary's womb, too, becomes part of this family line. (Theologian Caitlin Kim suggests that perhaps Mary, like Elizabeth, was part of the "tribe of Aaron," or the Levites, giving Jesus a priestly and royal heritage.[10])

To arrive at a clearer picture of the relationship, we may notice how, in the text of this antiphon, other kings *fall silent* before Christ. (Impossible here not to see the magi again, speechless with wonder at the stable.) This recalls the way that, throughout the history of Israel, the people brought into being one political order after another: orders that they often expected to be salvific. Yet salvation could not be found in any political order, not in any set of laws, not in any pressure group or in any merely human leader. Even the Ten Commandments – which are referenced in yesterday's antiphon, which have been given for our guidance, and which remain valid for Christians – taken on their own, lack the power to save. Only the embodiment of the Law, in the person of Jesus Christ, has this salvific power. Only he can, at one and the same time, lead, rule, and save.

Christ himself, in all of his human particularity united to his divine universality, is "a sign for the peoples" or a "signal for the nations". What is he signalling to us? The call is clear: "Repent, for the kingdom of heaven is at hand" (*Matt* 4:17).

---

[10] Caitlin Kennell Kim, *Was Mary of the House of David or Just Joseph?*, 16 July 2013: *https://bustedhalo.com/questionbox/was-mary-of-the-house-of-david-or-just-joseph*

This is why, both now and during the preparation for Easter that occurs in Lent, the Church prays the verse, "Prepare the way of the Lord" (*Isa* 40:3). We prepare the way precisely bringing our own history and embodied reality, whatever these may be, into relationship and alignment with the history and embodied reality of Christ's life and teaching. No one is barred, no one is dismissed, no one is held at a remove: "For as many as you as were baptised into Christ have put on Christ. There is neither Jew nor Greek, there is neither slave nor free, there is no male and female, for you are all one in Christ Jesus's" (*Gal* 3:27-28). This is not to say that our differences are erased, but instead that no characteristic of ours may limit the grace, the degree of God's life in us, we are able to receive. Nor does it mean that, subjectively, we may not experience tensions and obstacles: of course we will. These will differ according to our individual stories. But in order to extend his invitation to all, Christ needed to be born into a nation whose *individual story as a people* – their heritage, their central narrative – promised an Anointed One who would have power to lead and guide, rule and save.

It is worth taking this time to develop a deeper under-standing of the identity of Jesus Christ, since it does so much to explain our own identity in him through baptism and through our participation in the Eucharist. The sacramental life of the Church establishes our friendship, our common life, with Jesus. In this friendship, we become open to the indwelling of the Holy Trinity in our souls. We come in close contact. And since, as Fr James Brent has explained with reference to Aristotle and St Thomas,[11] a friend is another self, friendship with Jesus is how we become, in a certain sense, another Christ. This friendship is how we imitate Mary; it is how we bear Christ into the world. It is how the impossible becomes possible in us.

Christ's life in us is no mere metaphor. It is a living and active reality, which requires our conscious agency to reach its fulfilment. It is a gift that does not belong to us alone, but instead is given us for the sake of communal and personal love, in which we will find our own fulfilment and flourishing. Catholic writer Caryll Houselander reports that her reversion to the Church involved a mystical vision in which she saw every human being on the earth, without exception, as embodying a stage in the life of Christ. Some carried the infant Christ; some lived his active life; some rejoiced in him; some grieved in him. Some spoke his words to others; some bore his Cross. Even those in mortal sin still held a Christ-life that had died inside them, waiting for their repentance to allow his Resurrection to be enacted in them. Houselander writes of this experience as follows:

> I was in an underground train, a crowded train in which all sorts of people jostled together, sitting and strap-hanging – workers of every description going home at the end of the day. Quite suddenly I saw with my mind,

[11] Fr James Brent, O.P., "Freedom, Friendship, and the Good Life: Lessons from The Pandemic," lecture for the Thomistic Institute, 19th April 2021.

but as vividly as a wonderful picture, Christ in them all. But I saw more than that…. [B]ecause He was in them, and because they were here, the whole world was here too, here in this underground train….

It would be impossible to set down here all the implications of this "vision" of Christ in man; it altered the course of my life completely… I saw that is the will of Christ's love to…trust Himself to men, that He may be *their* gift to one another, that *they* may comfort Him in one another, give Him to each other. In this sense the ordinary life itself becomes sacramental, and every action of anyone at all has an eternal meaning.[12]

Without a doubt, this vision throws significant light on Houselander's idea, which we considered earlier, that every person is also in a certain way Mary, bearing Christ into the world. If we recognise her work, we also recognise his, since they are inseparable. As St Louis de Montfort wrote: "If we praise [Mary] or glorify her, she immediately praises and glorifies Jesus. As of old when St Elizabeth praised her, so now when we praise her and bless her, she sings: 'My soul doth magnify the Lord.'"[13] If we imitate one, we imitate the other. They are inseparable; and the image of the "root of Jesse," Christ's human lineage, hymns this inseparability in both physical and spiritual life.

---

[12] Caryll Houselander, *A Rocking-Horse Catholic* (London: Catholic Way Publishing, 2013), 106–107.

[13] St Louis de Montfort, *True Devotion to Mary* (Rockford, IL: TAN, 1985), 94.

O Clavis David

Gospel Acclamation:
*Key of David, who open the gates of the eternal
kingdom, come to liberate from prison the
captive who lives in darkness.*

Magnificat Antiphon:
*O key of David and sceptre of Israel, what you
open no one else can close again; what you close
no one can open. O come and lead the captive
from prison; free those who sit in darkness and
in the shadow of death.*

Reflection:

The imagery of this antiphon takes some work to unlock. To the degree that we may tend to resist the idea that the guidance of an authority is necessary to salvation, even more are we likely to struggle with this image of locked gates between us and the "eternal kingdom." To the extent that we are acculturated into a worldview that perceives God's laws as arbitrary, or secretly sourced in human invention, we will have trouble with this image. I will try to articulate our common trouble as follows.

The first problem: If the only thing standing between us and eternal freedom is a gate, why do we need a key to the gate? Why a gate at all? Why doesn't God just blow the gate off the hinges? Why does he seem to put up so many barriers, so many hedges, so many prescriptions and proscriptions, before we can access him? Shouldn't access to God be simple and direct and clean, a movement of the heart without practical obstacle? Isn't the process of growing into greater freedom, at its core, just a recognition that we are already radically free and cannot be forced into acts we do not agree with?

The second problem: How is the newborn, whose picture we are holding in our minds and who is the subject of all these antiphons, also somehow a *key* to anything at all? How do these helpless hands break us out of prison? To the extent that contemporary society *sees* newborns at all – for every new mother today knows in her bones that she, her newborn, and their shared needs are often socially invisible – it sees the newborn as a nexus of burdens, demands, obligations. And, in fairness, few new parents would describe having a newborn as freeing or liberating for themselves. Here again, we seem to have a mismatch in our imagery. (We might say, "This is difficult to *visualise*," in creative-writing workshop terms.) When God sets out to liberate us, why does he so often do this in ways that seem at first to bind us more tightly?

The answer to both problems lies not with God but with us. God is simple, but we are not. We experience creation as a multiplicity, a "blooming, buzzing confusion," – which, interestingly, is how philosopher William James described the experience of newborn children.[14] This is because we live *in medias res*, in the middle of the story, which God set in motion at the beginning of time. Our point of view about the whole of reality is limited; our perception can take us only so far. We may as well take a moment here to imagine the point of view of the newborn Jesus himself: fuzzy lights, warmth, chills; smells of hay and animals and milk, and of the barrier of cloth between his arms and the air; the blurry faces of Mary and Joseph and, farther away, of all those strange large bipeds his fragile human body knows only as *not-Mary* and *not-Joseph*. We don't often realise what a

---

[14] William James, *The Principles of Psychology* (Cambridge, MA: Harvard University Press, 1981), 462, original edition published in 1890.

breath-taking act of self-emptying, or what theologians call *kenosis*, this represents. We can tend to process, and maybe even psychologise, the Crucifixion as a piece of sublime heroics, as noble self-sacrifice for the good of others, but above all as an act of mature agency: something Jesus allowed to fulfil his Father's will. It's harder to imagine what a sacrifice of agency and even autonomy the Nativity itself represented. Why, if one could help it, as only God could have helped it, why choose such a total, radical limitation, such a willed reduction of infinite capacity? The ablation of one-eyed Odin is, forgive me the pun, not a patch on this. To accept our own radical, existential interdependence with others is, culturally and personally, far harder for many of us than any act of independent self-assertion could ever be. Here too, Jesus is our model, and all he must do to lead the way is consent to having a heartbeat. This may seem minimal, but it is no small thing.

To return, though, to considerations about our own point of view: We value our perception so deeply and so highly because clarity of mind and vision is the ground of our beloved agency and autonomy. Our perception even makes moral claims on us, as it truly *seems* to present things in their wholeness. It gives us light, but not all the light we need. If we steer by our solitary perception alone, we will find ourselves adrift. To clarify the confusion, we need boundaries. The more intense the human desire involved, the stronger and clearer the boundaries need to be.

This is why the Ten Commandments, and the habits and practices by which we conform to them, are not arbitrary but deeply ordered to our good. God's authority arises from his being the author of our human nature. He wrote his law into our hearts at our creation. Close attention to experience and to science, to every kind of possible human knowledge, can only in the end lead us closer to him, as "truth cannot contradict truth."[15] In making us the kind of creatures we are; not 'ghosts in a machine,' but matter-and-spirit unities, the kind of bodies we are, suspended inside the souls that animate them – in making us this way, God is not locking us into some miserable jail cell, from which we are only to be released at our physical death. The human body is a shelter, not a prison; a temple, not a cage.

In this situation, the Son-of-God-become-Man is an *interpretive* key as well as a literal one, capable of bringing us mental, emotional, and spiritual freedom as well as more immediate and obvious kinds of physical freedom. Contrary to our intuition, perhaps, this inner freedom must precede and inform the ever-greater degrees of external freedom to which it should lead everyone who embraces it. That maintaining this inner freedom requires our self-restraint should be no surprise to anyone who has ever pursued a discipline of any kind – sport, art, business, research, education, or any other human endeavour. If we follow such

---

[15] Pope St John Paul II, Address to the Pontifical Academy of Sciences, 1996, *https://www.vaticanobservatory.org/education/truth-cannot-contradict-truth-1996/*

disciplines, we discover things we *may not* do if we want to succeed, things that are incompatible with our goals.

In Catholic tradition, we describe sin as imprisonment, even as slavery. This is fraught language, conjuring images of cruelty and evil, and a history in which oppressors, many of them Christians, failed to honour the demands of human dignity for all, so it is worth taking time to ask what it really means. In what does this imprisonment, this slavery, consist? St. Paul touches the core of the dynamic when he writes, "I do not understand my own actions. For I do not do what I want, but I do the very thing I hate" (*Rom* 7:15). Few people reach adulthood without having at least some experience of this human tendency to 'self-destructive acts'. A still more vivid way of looking at this question, specifically, of looking at the positive vision of human freedom Catholicism proposes instead – is shaped by the ideal of holy poverty, embraced by generations of saints. This ideal recognises that whenever we put our own desires first, we tend to enslave ourselves to our own appetites. Turned in on themselves, our real needs become distended with bloat, distorted by accretions, until we now feel we 'need' things we once only wished for and come to crave things that sicken and weaken us. In this paradox we see that those who oppress others are often, themselves, at least equally trapped and oppressed by their own tendency towards evil, expressed in self-centeredness. Bound by their own extraneous and exorbitant demands to be served, to be pleased, and to have their sweeping visions carried out at any cost, they cannot even access the spiritual freedom that remains available to those they oppress. Without offering others real freedom, it is impossible to attain one's own liberation.

By contrast, holy poverty does not mean destitution; it is, instead, a willingness to be satisfied with sufficiency, what author Haley Stewart has called "the grace of enough." Religious orders and consecrated persons have long instantiated this ideal, and many throughout history have made a virtue of necessity by finding ways to thrive on fewer resources than most of us would consider liveable. This might seem like a digression, but it is relevant because the Holy Family was almost certainly among this multitude of those who have made their way through the world on just enough. Scholars have pointed for evidence to the two turtledoves offered by Mary and Joseph on the occasion of Jesus's circumcision in the Temple, in place of the more elaborate sacrifice usually brought by wealthy families. As a working artisan, Joseph would have earned a liveable and respectable income, but he would not have been affluent. And as an adult, after giving up his own workshop for his ministry, Jesus had "nowhere to lay his head" (*Matt* 8:20), famously telling his disciples to pack nothing more for travel than a staff and a pair of sandals – no food, money, or extra clothing allowed (cf. *Matt* 10:9-10).

While Christ does not call everyone to such total austerity, it remains tragic and needless to let so many in our society be deprived of daily needs, while others indulge in overwhelming excess. Justice calls us to find ways of being attentive to the needs of others. Wendell Berry asserts that, in order to establish justice and preserve resources for the future, the privileged "must achieve the character and acquire the skills to live much poorer than we do."[16] Thoreau, disciple of secular monasticism, writes: "A man is rich in proportion to the number of things which he can afford to let alone."[17] This line of thought finds its consonances in the Christian tradition, stemming from the examples of Joseph, Mary, and Jesus themselves: When we put the common good first and choose to live simply in terms of meeting our individual needs without excess, we find ourselves more free than when we are weighed down by literal tons of possessions that require maintenance, waste that ruins nature for future generations, and useless troves of luxuries that may amuse but cannot benefit us in the long term. Freedom, by contrast, comes only with the possession of "treasure in the heavens that does not fail, where no thief approaches and no moth destroys" (*Luke* 12:33).

In the language of faith, by contrast, the accomplishment of freedom is the attainment of a vision of the way God intended us to be free. Without our works of freedom,

---

[16] Wendell Berry, commencement address at the College of the Atlantic in Bar Harbor, Maine, 1989, quoted in full at *https://www.teachthought.com/education/shifting-from-ed-reform-to-classroom-reform-wendell-berry*.

[17] Henry David Thoreau, *Walden* (Boston: Ticknor & Fields, 1854), 89.

which are linked to our works of kindness to others, our faith in that vision is dead (cf. *James* 2:14-17). At the same time, paradoxically, this vision, this freedom, always keeps its ultimate nature as a gift, a grace. Under our own power alone, we are completely incapable of ever perfectly fulfilling it. However much effort we put into the work of kindness, our ability to perform generosity and the very things we give are always granted to us. No action of ours, no lifetime of actions, can ever fully deserve such fulfilment.

All the merit is on God's side, but God is a better and more generous giver than any human person can be. He does not attach strings. What he gives us, he gives us as our own. He will offer us all the grace we need, but he will never force us to co-operate with it. If we choose to misuse our freedom, we will miss the mark, and we will lose liberty and possibly even life itself. On the contrary, if we put our freedom to work for the good in a spirit of wholehearted love, we will find ourselves ever more deeply involved in kinds of freedom we never expected, freedoms *from* and freedoms *for*: freedom from hatred, from falsehood, from fear, from insatiable desire; freedom for excellence, for peace, for joy, for "the grace of enough."

How does the infant Christ, born into our lives and suddenly seeming to make a thousand new demands on us, involve us in these freedoms? We could ask this question another way, like the riddle it is: When is a newborn also a key? When he is an *interpretive* key: when what he stands for, what he instantiates, unlocks a prison in our minds. When the service of his needs – which present themselves to us as the needs of the people in our lives – liberates what is better in us and casts away what is worse. When he opens the door of our self-centeredness, a trap whose gate only ever locks from the inside, and invites us to walk out into our authentic strength. When he breaks us out of the prison of egotistical desire by transforming desire itself. When he gives us the power and liberty to be generous because God is generous, patient because God is patient, and loving because God is loving. He does all this most completely through his own Passion, Death, and Resurrection, but his birth sets the possibility of these events in motion; even in his infancy, his Incarnation already involves him in the work of redemption and us in the freedom of the children of God. If this liberty paradoxically binds us, it does so as a security against the dangers of self-absorption and self-deception. These are dangers to which no one is immune. As much as we are protected from them, to that same extent we can truly exercise our fullest freedom.

O Oriens

Gospel Acclamation:
Morning star, radiance of eternal light, sun of justice, come and enlighten those who live in darkness and in the shadow of death.

Magnificat Antiphon:
O Rising Sun, you are the splendour of eternal light and the sun of justice. O come and enlighten those who sit in darkness and the shadow of death.

Reflection:

We know that Christ is "the light of the world" (*John* 8:12), the "way, the truth, and the life" (*John* 14:6). We know these words, we have heard them so many times they may land like a bromide – flat and tasteless – but I wonder if it isn't that the salt has lost its savour, but rather that we have lost our sensitivity to it. I wonder if we don't tend to hold these words at arm's length because on some level we feel threatened by their implications. If we truly allow ourselves to accept these realities, to follow the line of logic they lead us down, then no longer can we steer 'by our lights' alone. Christ is "the true light, which gives light to everyone," and at Christmastide he is "coming into the world" (*John* 1:9) – and while other lights may shine alongside Christ's light, reflecting it or glowing with brilliance ultimately borrowed from it, we cannot pretend that these other lights can give us sufficient guidance by themselves. The question is not so much: Where is the light coming from? We know the answer already. If we see truth and light, we can be sure that its source is found in Christ, even if the path of refraction remains mysterious to us. The question is, instead: Is our vision sufficiently clear to receive the fullness of the light, or are we harbouring shades that will block it out? "The eye is the lamp of the body. So, if your eye is healthy, your whole body will be full of light, but if your eye is bad, your whole body will be full of darkness. If then the light in you is darkness, how great is the darkness?" (*Matt* 6:22-23). Jesus is, of course, using a metaphor: he does not mean that literal bodily visual disease can possibly block our spiritual vision, but that our inner vision can be obscured by false attachments. The link to yesterday's antiphon, with its consideration of moral vision and the major obstacle to moral vision posed when we choose to "sit in darkness" (i.e. sin), stands out clearly. If a shadow stands between us and the light, if our out-of-sync attachments to material things and desires block our clarity of thought and therefore our practice of freedom, we will struggle and suffer needlessly until we break free, once again able to see and move untrammelled.

Not unrelated: If you spend abundant time on the internet – and today, that not only describes most of us, it is a comic understatement – you are already aware that, every year around this date, a spate of articles crops up claiming to prove that Christmas is "really" a pagan festival, since it occurs around the time of the winter solstice and bears some historical relationship to the ancient Roman festival of Saturnalia, a wildly debauched midwinter festival, which the cultural celebration of Christmas allegedly replaced.

It's understandable how the rise of interest in pagan practices attracts many who feel alienated from the natural world and from the cycles of creation. However, we can feel confident that whatever good dwells in these natural cycles also finds its reflection in the liturgical cycles of Christian practice. There is no need to be surprised or scandalised that the timing of Christmas in the Church calendar coincides with the winter solstice, the moment at which light begins to overtake darkness in the natural world. The early Christians were well aware of the symbolism. Though many were former pagans, determined to efface the mistakes of their past, they did not reject this natural symbolism but rather chose consciously to make use of it: to baptise rather than to banish. Remember, grace builds on nature; grace does not destroy nature. Our delighted and longing anticipation of light's return to the world, far from being suspect, is deeply rooted in our embodied creaturehood, which the authentic mind of the Church honours and values.

For Christ's light is more than mere natural light – without which, though it is only a created thing, our created bodies could not live. The metaphor is an exquisite one, however, as Christ is the light without which our souls cannot sustain life. He is no mere metonymy for the sun, in the sense of Apollo or Huitzilopochtli or Ra, dwelling somehow 'in' the sun in a panentheistic sense. Instead he is the light of the soul, "the light of the world" in spirit and in truth. He is the "splendour of eternal light" and "the sun of justice," the Word who is God and who is with God from all time, as we read in the first chapter of John's Gospel. His justice must be linked to his light, as the clarity of its truth is what sets us free.

Translator Jacob Riyeff offers the following meditation, translated from an Old English poem on this antiphon, which invites us to consider how the light of Christ casts aside the work of falsehood, "scatters the proud in the thoughts of their hearts," and "fill[s] the hungry with good things" (*Luke* 1:51, 53):

> You illumine all times outside time,
> resplendent beyond the stars…
> So your own works pray in their weakness
> that you might send the gleaming Sun
> and come yourself to illumine those lingering
> here, covered with smoke and unceasing
> night, enduring the shadow of death….
> So we give thanks unceasingly for this wonder:
> that the God of victories would give us himself.[18]

Once more, it is worth noticing what complete nonsense many pagan religions might have found this idea. For humanity's earliest civilisations, gods were thought to live at an impossible remove from humans. The boundary between the human and the divine could never be crossed. Gods were not thought to be models for human behaviour so much as capricious reflections of human cruelty and lust and aggression. As far as salvation, it came from human effort if it came at all: the heroes who were deified or invited to live on Olympus were, without exception, extraordinary scions of noble families, often said to be half-god themselves in

---

[18] From "O Radiant Dawn," in *O Shining Light*, Jacob and Mamie Riyeff, with translations by Jacob Riyeff (Leominster, Herefordshire: Gracewing, 2020), 37–39.

origin, who performed outstanding deeds. The myths held up such acts in contradistinction to the mundane lives most people live of necessity. While later philosophers would resist this movement towards glorifying heroism, preferring instead to lift up acts of virtue more accessible to a wider range of people, the seeds of the *übermenschian* attitude would remain in the stories, and that attitude continues to affect us to this day.

The ancient model offered the ordinary person basically no hope, except for the Pelagian, bootstrapper's 'hope' Hercules offered the wagon driver in the fable: "The gods help those who help themselves." Under this dispensation, nothing could be done about those situations so common in human experience in which our effort takes us only so far, in which the basic parameters of our plight either cannot be changed or can only be changed with extreme measures that may or may not improve matters, indeed, that may not even be within our individual power, acting alone. Classical fatalism, for all its exterior beauty, offered no way to make sense of pain, oppression, or betrayal: no respite for situations in which, at least in the short term, the only freedoms left to us are interior.

Christ turned these situations inside out by entering into one of them himself. The "light of the world" entered into the darkness, "and the darkness has not overcome it" (*John* 1:5).

An absolute innocent, the one person ever to live who was as clean of heart as an adult as he had been in his earliest childhood, Christ allowed himself to be treated as a criminal. He gave up his health and youth and strength, everything contemporary culture worships, to be assaulted and damaged and destroyed – not out of any twisted belief, such as we sometimes hold in our pain, that those who suffer have somehow earned their ill treatment, but, instead, in the knowledge that humanity was created good and needed to be set free by extreme measures.

His one outstanding moment of self-gift would become faith's anchor for future generations and would give its own meaning to every act performed in conformity with it. "For our sake he made him to be sin who knew no sin" (*2 Cor* 5:21), not in the sense that he ever chose evil, but instead that he took on the full burden of human evil and, in allowing it to destroy his body, allowed evil itself to self-destruct. He showed us how the power of fear over us can be broken: "do not fear those who kill the body but cannot kill the soul" (*Matt* 10:28); we can count on our access to God's saving power, as long as we do not consent to acts whose choice would destroy our souls. That Christ chose exactly this kind of suffering, that he refused to perform the evil that would have been the public denial of his own true goodness, may be some comfort to those who have had no choice and no agency in the evil that was done to them by others. The deepest practice of agency people can practice in such situations might be found in standing firm against the idea that the pain they have suffered has somehow corrupted or made them evil, in holding fast instead to the goodness that lives at the deepest levels of their being – for this goodness is surely Christ in them, and it is therefore Christ who has suffered in them, with them, and ultimately for their salvation: "For you will not abandon my soul to Sheol [hell], or let your holy one see corruption" (*Ps* 16:10). The deeper the darkness around us, the more we must trust in, and hope for, the returning light.

O Rex Gentium

Gospel Acclamation:
*King of the peoples and cornerstone of the Church,
come and save man whom you made from the dust
of the earth.*

Magnificat Antiphon:
*O King whom all the peoples desire, you are the
cornerstone which makes all one. O come and save
man whom you made from clay.*

Reflection:

The kingship of Christ, which we first considered in the antiphon "*O Adonai*," recurs here with more insistence. After considering what kind of king Christ is, and how he begins to rule in our lives, we can see that his Incarnation resolves the tensions that run through our relationships with divine authority and divine intimacy. Wherever Christ is king – which is not necessarily wherever people pay him lip service, but wherever he is really allowed to reign – false oppositions are reconciled, necessary boundaries are strengthened while needless walls crumble, and all divisions, fractures, or separations that do not please God are healed. Christ "makes all one," not by erasing difference, but by putting an end to discrimination, disregard, and disrespect. He soothes the pain of those who suffer and lifts them up to act worthily of their dignity. He not only calls for the repentance of those who harm others, he heals the woundedness that led to such unrighteous behaviour.

Once more, then, God is restored to the place he had in the Garden of Eden when he spoke familiarly with Adam. He speaks to us in and through a human nature he shares with us: even when he walked on the earth, he "needed no one to bear witness about [humanity], for he himself knew what was in" human hearts (*John* 2:25). Once more he walks beside us, in our hearts, as he once walked on earth in the body for a brief time.

Today he walks beside us in the lives of all those who live his teachings, in the Sacraments of the Church, and above all in the Eucharist, where he is really present, Body, Blood, Soul, and Divinity: "When he was at table with them, he took the bread and blessed and broke it and gave it to them. And their eyes were opened, and they recognised him…. [T]hey said to each other, 'Did not our hearts burn within us…while he opened to us the Scriptures?'" (*Luke* 24:30-32)

At the same time, at this stage in history, Jesus Christ sits in glory at the right hand of God the Father. He sees our hearts: he always honours the intended wholeness and the innate goodness given to each person. This is why he is depicted in the tradition as the one who judges, why he is considered the only one who may judge: he is the only one capable of seeing the full picture. Yet in the Gospel of John, he even says: "I did not come to judge the world, but to save the world" (*John* 12:47). The verse goes on to unfold how Christ, as light, shines into the world not as judgement but as hope. Those who close their eyes to the light lose the ability to comprehend it. Christ's word is the only thing capable of showing us credibly how some acts, some habits, are not worthy of our human dignity, as they do not lead us to lives of full flourishing. He calls on us to turn aside from anything that prevents our flourishing and that of others in our families and societies. He asks us to change – sometimes in ways that strike at what we think of as our roots, sometimes in ways whose cost runs high – but all of this change is only in service of the fullness of our potential and that of others. Christ as King sees and pursues the whole picture of the common good in the Church, in the world, and in the interior of each soul. He wants, most incredibly of all, not to see us bent down as abject subjects, but walking close beside him and looking at the same object: God the Father, the source of all goodness and truth and beauty.

This is how C.S. Lewis famously describes the posture of friendship: two people walking side by side, looking at the same truth together, in wonder. And Christ himself says, "I have called you friends" (*John* 15:15). And who is this friend we have, other than the one who made us "from clay" or, as Genesis has it, from dust? "Without him was not any thing made that was made" (*John* 1:3); "before I formed you in the womb I knew you" (*Jer* 1:5). Our being has its source in him and finds its only hope in him.

So here again, as in the antiphon "*O Radix Jesse*," we call upon Jesus to come and save us – this time not only in the communal voice of the People of God, but in the voice of each one of us, individually, personally: "Out of the depths I cry to you, O Lord! O Lord, hear my voice!" (*Ps* 130:1-2). This time we call upon him in the fullness of his power, in the fullness of restored divine friendship, and as ones who have been given by grace every right to call – the way children have every right to call upon their parents to have their needs met.

The sound is still more intense. The need is still more demanding. Why is he not with us yet? Why has he not been with us before now? Is it possible that he is here already, has been here all along, and we have not yet perceived him, even as he was with the disciples and they did not know him? But how can we say that God wants to be with us when he so often appears absent from our experience? Could it be that he is with us all along, but that we are absent from him – like St Augustine, looking for God everywhere except where he most properly rules?

O Emmanuel

Gospel Acclamation:
Emmanuel, our king and lawgiver, come and save us, Lord our God.

Magnificat Antiphon:
O Emmanuel, you are our king and judge, the One whom the peoples await and their Saviour. O come and save us, Lord our God.

Reflection:

This antiphon speaks what is, in the end, each human heart's deepest desire: to have God with it, to be with God, to be in God, and to know God's indwelling. This is precisely what the name *Emmanuel* means: *God with us*. To accomplish this being with us, Jesus came to earth and inhabited a human body. For this reason "the Word became flesh and dwelt among us" (*John* 1:14). The story of our redemption springs from no other root than love. Even more than we long to be embraced, ennobled, transformed, God longs to embrace and ennoble and transform us.

In human terms, this makes either all the sense in the world or, perhaps, absolutely no sense at all. Why would the Creator of all things, perfectly happy in himself and with no need of human life or a created world, not only decide to create souls inside bodies, but to take on this embodied, ensouled creaturehood for himself? If what God wants is souls, what purpose is served by all these querulous, problematic, high-maintenance bodies we carry around the world with us? Would *we* have wanted to become incarnate, if we had been God? The idea of substitutionary atonement is next to impossible to wrap our minds around, because it lies outside the logic of human psychology unaided by grace. Even under the influence of grace, how many of us would ever do it, knowing that to do it completely would mean indescribable suffering?

God, fortunately for us, does not have the kind of cold clockwork heart we humans often imagine for him – an assumption that has more to do with the kind of heart we tend to carry around inside ourselves than it does with the heart of God. Instead, *his* heart yearns towards us. The more we suffer, the closer to us he longs to be. The more we suffer, the more he is with us, in a mysterious yet real way. The saints describe this experience, but it is not an experience restricted to saints alone. It is there for the asking, for all of us who know what it is to be "mourning and weeping in this vale of tears." "For one will scarcely die for a righteous person – though perhaps for a good person one would dare even to die, but God shows his love for us in that while we were still sinners, Christ died for us" (*Rom* 5:6-8).

If we believe what Caryll Houselander saw in her mystical vision of Christ – alive, at work, asleep, or dead in every single human soul – we also see that this life of Christ is, in one sense, always as close as our own hearts. In another sense, though, we are not one with Christ until we receive the Sacraments. Until then, we lack access to that deeper friendship with Christ in which he is 'another self' to us. To put this another way, Christ desires a certain reciprocity with us. Our concerns are always his, but the circle is not complete until we make his concerns ours. When we step forward into this friendship, always first moved by grace, he then becomes our "king and lawgiver" in a way that parallels the presence of God given to the first humans, who walked 'with God' in Eden. He then dwells directly in our hearts, pulling us ever more completely into the life of the Trinity. He then guides and leads us from within, in close and compassionate conversation with us. This conversation, which is what prayer consists of, begins now and extends into eternity. It proves the reality of the bold statement made by St Catherine of Siena: that Jesus is like a 'bridge' connecting heaven and earth, by which "the earth of your humanity is joined to the greatness of the Deity."[19]

Prayer and the Sacraments place us on this bridge, a path that, as St Catherine reports, God calls each one of us individually to pursue: "It is not enough, in order that you should have life, that My Son should have made you this bridge, unless you walk thereon."[20] On the bridge that is Christ himself, the bridge that is his Incarnation, Passion, Death, and Resurrection, perennially made present in the holy sacrifice of the Mass, no one walks alone. No one is saved alone; we always need the Church, the one community that is also a communion with Christ, because while he was on earth he united himself to it. When we make God's concerns our own, we always, inescapably, become concerned with our neighbour's wellbeing, too. For God is equally concerned with the welfare of every single person – and one reason for so much suffering is that,

---

[19] *The Dialogue of St Catherine*, ch. 2, paragraph 8, IntraText concordance edition (Eulogos, 2007): *http://www.intratext.com/IXT/ENG0139/_PH.HTM#3W*

[20] Ibid.

although God is equally concerned with all, each one of us is mostly concerned with self. Instead of bringing forth what we have in us to bear, we frequently choose to escape into the distractions of comfort, pleasure, or (let's admit it) self-righteous indignation that *those people over there* haven't changed yet. Let us not deceive ourselves. The world, our relationships, our institutions, our environment, will *never change until we do*. And only God can change us: and he can do this only from within.

How fortunate for us, then, that he became so small: so small, small enough to fit inside Mary's womb (*non horruisti virginis uterum*). Smaller than a mustard seed, smaller than faith itself: precisely as small as a blastocyst – a microscopic, pre-embryonic human – allowing himself to quietly implant and to grow. How fortunate for us that he allowed himself to grow, not in a miraculous acceleration of progress, but at precisely the pace that we ourselves grow. Nine months after the Annunciation, how fortunate for us that he was born: as purple and slick, as silky and fragile and fragrant, as wonderful, as terrible, as awe-inspiring, as any couple's first baby: no more and no less so, to look at him from the outside, than any other newborn. And yet this newborn was God. How fully he 'commands what he gives and gives what he commands,' in asking us to 'love God with all our heart and all our soul and all our strength.' How easy to love, how completely lovable, he makes himself in this Incarnation: how unthreatening, how gentle, how vulnerable: "O happy fault, o necessary sin of Adam, that merited for us so great a Redeemer."[21]

And all the while, whether we have never left the path, have wandered away from it for a time, or have only begun to discover it, he loves each one of us as his own, only child. He is always with us, within us, waiting to be welcomed, perhaps waiting to be noticed. He awaits only our openness, our willingness, in order to be born into the world once more.

That image of the infant Christ waiting to be born brings us to one other thing I find in this antiphon, beyond the ideas of impending reunion and restoration: namely, a poetic turn. Often found towards the end of a story or sonnet, this literary device restates or recombines an idea in a way that helps us see it still more clearly. Catholic writer and scholar Randy Boyagoda finds a poetic turn "Halfway through the Hail Mary," a silence between the two main phrases of the prayer, which he reads as signifying the birth of Christ.[22] The poetic turn in the O Antiphons, I suggest, takes place here at their ending and signifies not the actual birth of Christ but the moments just before it: the stage known to every labouring mother as *transition*.

Anyone who has ever witnessed or experienced labour knows that transition is intense. Instinct takes over, and

---

[21] "Exultet," from the Easter Vigil, in *The Roman Missal*.

[22] Randy Boyagoda, "Halfway Through the Hail Mary," in *First Things*, December 2002: *https://www.firstthings.com/article/2002/12/halfway-through-the-hail-mary?fbclid=IwAR0Svo0wUDiRMg-dxczv2LQKia1flKUOSt4Bi1_q8wKwJWulAQOM-LB_8tU.*

whatever is deepest in the heart finds itself coming up to the surface. It is a moment marked by one purpose: the child must be born, and the mother must find a way. She must put aside whatever stands in between her current state and the success of her effort. You and I and everyone else reading this page are breathing right now because she succeeded.

The urgency of that moment may often be used as an analogy, but those who have done it know it compares to nothing else. The technical term for the physical process that, quite literally, crowns the endeavour – *foetal ejection reflex* – does not begin to cover the human experience of giving birth. It is totalising, requiring in that moment all the person has, all she is: all her heart, all her soul, all her strength. Birth, like the story of salvation, is eucatastrophic.

Do we feel an intensity like this in our desire to bring Christ into the world anew? If not, what might be standing in between us and that intensity? How might we begin to put that aside, to make room for our Lord in our lives, in our very bodies – giving new meaning to Isaiah's "In the wilderness prepare the way of the Lord, make straight in the desert a highway for our God" (*Isa* 40:3)?

"*O Emmanuel*" captures in compressed form every idea that has been present in the preceding six antiphons. Its brevity suggests that there is not much time left to say what needs to be said. We had better say it now, while we still have breath left! Christmas is almost here: the breathless push into new life is upon us.

Come Lord Jesus

Throughout this series of reflections, we have held up a set of images – leader, lawgiver, root, key, sunlight, king – in juxtaposition to the image of an infant born into poverty: a child who, we know, is also God the Son, God with us in history, in our own time, and in the future. We have considered how it is that this child fits into these images; how it may be that, working in our world's characteristic modes of thought, we may have trouble relating to each image; and how we can begin to think and feel our way around that trouble into a deeper understanding. But a central part of our work together remains undone, and this is the time to do it.

At the outset I told you that I am not a consecrated person or a trained theologian. All I have to bring to this work is the self I have been given and the training this self has received. At heart I am a writer, someone sensitive to the sound and sense of language, and an editor, someone unable to leave well enough alone when it comes to the structure of language. Perhaps it is this inability to leave well enough alone that leads me to want to pull apart the structure of these antiphons, to ask why they are made the way they are.

In particular: Why not leave off the "O"? Why is the *shape* of this sound important? Why is its form particularly fitting to the prayer we need to pray? I must confess now that I find this "O" irritatingly open, unbearably urgent, almost embarrassing in the depth of its vulnerability. It strikes me this way despite my knowing that the "O" is often used in classical literature as a form of address, when calling upon deities or muses to ask for inspiration; Shakespeare, too, puts it to good use in his plays and poetry in the context of a range of human emotions. Maybe this is why I have left this one aspect of the text more or less unaddressed until now: The "O" of the O Antiphons could seem either literary, an unneeded decorative flourish, or overemotional, melodramatic. In literature we could more easily explain it – or explain it away. But in the liturgy, nothing is without a purpose. What is this all-too-human sound doing here?

For it is precisely its location in the liturgy that makes this sound unaccountable, difficult to deal with. *Why* should it be so difficult? It seems consonant, after all, with the cry of a labouring mother, which is echoed in the cry of the labouring Church, working to bring forth Christ into the world anew. Even more appropriately, it is used here to call upon the One God in tones that we can almost hear him using to answer us, in the vowel-laden cry of the newborn

Christ, mouth circling open in questioning call for the answer of Mary's encircling arms.

This appropriateness, almost too easy, is where I locate the difficulty: How can we identify this 'oversound' of cries of vulnerability and need with the power and decisiveness of Mary's voice as we hear it in the *Magnificat*? One possibility is that it may circle back to all we have been saying about the paradox of the Incarnation. As humans, we can tend to struggle with one or another aspect of this paradox, depending on our personal dispositions. Either we celebrate 'messiness' at the expense of clarity, or we insist on order at the expense of wonder. Rather, the Incarnation is the source and summit of the classic Catholic both/and dynamic, the 'great *et et.*' To downplay or deny either part is to diminish, if not lose, the whole.

A confession: Temperamentally, at least in my adult life, I tend to champion the unpopular value of order. (If you ask my mother, she will tell you this was not a noticeable tendency of my childhood.) Although I am now a mother of four, I can sometimes number myself among those who question whether the cries of children *really belong* in the sanctuary during Mass. This may be understandable as a wishful longing for a moment's silence, but if it goes much beyond this, it is open to serious criticism. God insists on becoming little and familiar and easy to love – and demanding, in the face of my insistence that God remains distant and remote and majestic – and unconcerned with my ilk. A distant God is, though more difficult to love, simpler to deal with, to bracket, to dismiss for the moment, if I am not in the mood to think about the vastness of eternity, or if I am busy with some plan of my own into which the incursion of the Divine feels inconvenient. If I can keep God conceptual and vague, I need not change my habits or my attachments. I can 'play small' with God, reminding him not to ask too much of me because after all I'm so insignificant, instead of reckoning with the true parameters of my life or facing the reality of how I waste his gifts of time and my own potential. I can entertain the temptation to despise the idea of offering God my days and hours and minutes, the small but necessary acts that bore me as well as the grand gestures my sense of drama would strongly prefer. I can make excuses, lying to myself that as I'm so useless, incapable of offering God anything worth having, I need not make the effort to offer him anything at all.

At the same time, like a good many people today, I am well educated in the 'God-helps-those-who-help-themselves' school of devotion. I tend to like showing off my accomplishments to God – accomplishments whose value I wildly overinflate, not unlike a child bringing home fingerpaint smears from school for her mother to clip to the fridge. And at times when I have few or no accomplishments to bring, I tend to forget I have anything else God might want or find useful. I tend not to expect anything I haven't worked for and to discount the value of anything I haven't earned. (I told my spiritual mentor that this tendency was 'semi-Pelagian' because I wanted her to be impressed with two things: one, that I was fluent at owning up to foolishness, and two, that I knew that Pelagianism was a belief in self-salvation by nature without grace. She didn't turn an eyelash: good for her.)

Such disproportions involve what our tradition calls the pride of timidity, and that pride is as much opposed as arrogance to the genuine humility of the *Magnificat*, whose spirit reverberates throughout the O Antiphons.

To explain Mary's spirit of humility to us, who do not come to it connaturally, Caryll Houselander in her classic work *The Reed of God* turns to images to explain it. It should not surprise us by now that the images Houselander turns to are those of round, hollow, open things. The three she chooses to focus most closely upon are those of the reed (or flute), used for song, the chalice, for sacrifice, and the bird's nest, for security: all three things Mary is given by God and offers in return to him from her own being. With these images, Houselander reminds us that 'form follows function' – that shape and material relate closely to purpose. Each created thing, including each person, Houselander says, is formed by experience and circumstance into a shape uniquely suited for a purpose. But we cover and obscure these shapes, overwhelm ourselves with physical and mental and emotional clutter, until we can no longer discern their original capacities:

Those who complain…of the emptiness of their lives are usually afraid to allow space or silence or pause in their lives. They dread space, for they want material things crowded together, so that there will always be something to lean on for support. They dread silence, because they do not want to hear their own pulses beating out the seconds of their life… Such emptiness is very different from that still, shadowless ring of light round which our being is circled, making a shape which in itself is an absolute promise of fulfilment.

The shape of the "O" sound, like that of Houselander's "ring of light," the way she pictures our innate power of contemplation, is beautifully suited to singing of human need, desire, and uncluttered emptiness: all in us that has the potential to bear fruit. It shines at communicating prayers that dwell in us beyond the power of language to articulate:

For we know that the whole creation has been groaning together in the pains of childbirth until now. And not only the creation, but we ourselves, who have the firstfruits of the Spirit, groan inwardly as we wait eagerly for adoption…for the redemption of our bodies. For in this hope we were saved…. We do not know how to pray as we ought, but the Holy Spirit intercedes for us with groanings too deep for words (*Rom* 8:22-26).

The series of O Antiphons, then, paradoxically challenges me, because it speaks for me, speaks in my place, when I would so much rather speak for myself: but it says so much better than I do what I most need to say. In this way it accepts something in me that I don't easily accept in myself: my own emptiness before God, my need for his grace and gifts to fill my life. Left to my own devices, I will clutter up my nest like a magpie with any junk that floats into my orbit, trying to use it to disguise my own essential form – a disguise I am desperate to create.

The Great O Antiphons, by contrast, represent a piece of the liturgy which, without having to change it or myself, I can appropriate as my own: one that does not put up barriers to me but accepts me, as I am, in my created reality in its entirety.

Maybe this very ease has sent me looking for whatever seems most difficult in the O Antiphons, whatever in them might go against intuition. I expect, and almost want, the liturgy to be distancing, othering. I want it to resist me, to demand something difficult from me. A liturgy I could wholly comprehend, one I could just as easily have invented myself, would be one I could not easily surrender to. We all long for this divine Otherness, and the liturgy is a natural place to bring this longing. What a comical surprise to find there, instead, the God of infinities falling over himself to meet me exactly where I am.

The Magnificat

My soul magnifies the Lord,
and my spirit rejoices in God my Saviour,
for he has looked on the humble estate of his servant.
For behold, from now on all generations will
*   call me blessed;*
for he who is mighty has done great things for me,
and holy is his name.
And his mercy is for those who fear him
from generation to generation.
He has shown strength with his arm;
he has scattered the proud in the thoughts of
*   their hearts;*
he has brought down the mighty from their thrones
and exalted those of humble estate;
he has filled the hungry with good things,
and the rich he has sent away empty.
He has helped his servant Israel,
in remembrance of his mercy,
as he spoke to our fathers,
to Abraham and his offspring forever.

(Luke 1:46-55)

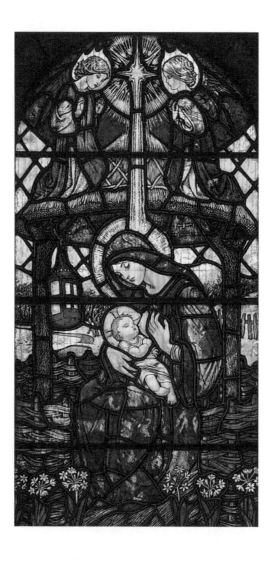